W9-BKJ-536

DISASTERS
PEOPLE IN PERIL

FORTY-NINE MINUTES OF MADNESS

THE COLUMBINE HIGH SCHOOL SHOOTING

Judy L. Hasday

Enslow Publishers, Inc.
40 Industrial Road
Box 398
Berkeley Heights, NJ 07922
USA
http://www.enslow.com

Dedicated to the memory of all those young students who have lost their lives through senseless violence

Original edition published as *Columbine High School Shooting: Student Violence* in 2002.

Library of Congress Cataloging-in-Publication Data

Hasday, Judy L., 1957–
  Forty-nine minutes of madness : the Columbine High School shooting / Judy L. Hasday.
    p. cm. — (Disasters-people in peril)
  Rev. ed. of: Columbine High School Shooting, c2002.
  Includes bibliographical references and index.
  Summary: "Examines the tragic shooting at Columbine High School on April 20, 1999, including detailed reports of the horrific events, background on the killers, and the aftermath of the shooting"—Provided by publisher.
  ISBN 978-0-7660-4013-7
  1. School shootings—Colorado—Littleton—Juvenile literature. 2. Columbine High School (Littleton, Colo.)—Juvenile literature. 3. Columbine High School Massacre, Littleton, Colo., 1999—Juvenile literature. I. Hasday, Judy L., 1957– Columbine High School shooting. II. Title.
  LB3013.33.C6H38 2013
  373.17'820978882—dc23

2011045276

Future editions:
Paperback ISBN 978-1-4644-0111-4
ePUB ISBN 978-1-4645-1018-2
PDF ISBN 978-1-4646-1018-9

Printed in the United States of America

032012 Lake Book Manufacturing, Inc., Melrose Park, IL

10 9 8 7 6 5 4 3 2 1

To Our Readers: We have done our best to make sure all Internet addresses in this book were active and appropriate when we went to press. However, the author and the publisher have no control over and assume no liability for the material available on those Internet sites or on other Web sites they may link to. Any comments or suggestions can be sent by e-mail to comments@enslow.com or to the address on the back cover.

♻ Enslow Publishers, Inc., is committed to printing our books on recycled paper. The paper in every book contains 10% to 30% post-consumer waste (PCW). The cover board on the outside of each book contains 100% PCW. Our goal is to do our part to help young people and the environment too!

Illustration Credits: AP Images, p. 23; AP Images / Ed Andrieski, pp. 6, 20, 29, 31, 33, 38, 41, 42; AP Images / Eric Gay, pp. 1, 36; AP Images / Glen Martin, p. 18; AP Images / HO, pp. 12, 34; AP Images / Jefferson County Sherriff's Department, pp. 9, 24; AP Images / KCNC-TV Denver, p. 27; AP Images / KUSA-TV, p. 16; AP Images / Laura Rauch, p. 4.

Cover Illustration: AP Images / Eric Gay (A participant holds up a sign reading "Stop the Madness" during a memorial service on April 25, 1999, at Columbine High School).

CONTENTS

Rachel Ruth (left), Rhianna Cheek (center), and Mandi Annibel, three sophomores from Columbine High School, console each other at a vigil service honoring the shooting victims on April 21, 1999, a day after the murderous assault at their school.

CHAPTER ONE

"JUDGMENT DAY"

AT ONE TIME, LITTLETON, COLORADO, was just a small prairie town located at the foothills of the Rocky Mountains. In the mid-1800s, gold prospectors and traders occupied this area around present-day Denver, Colorado's state capital. Whether they found their fortunes or not, many gold seekers decided to settle permanently in this relatively undeveloped territory. Over time, more people came to make their homes in the area. Soon, Denver and the surrounding towns grew into thriving communities.

The town of Littleton is located just a few miles southwest of Denver. In 1999, it had about forty thousand residents.[1] Most are middle-income families, living in attractive homes on quiet cul-de-sacs. In Littleton, people do not bother to lock their doors. At Littleton's Columbine High School, the school motto is engraved over an arch in the hallway: "The finest kids in America pass through these halls."[2] To their horror, the residents of Littleton would discover that two of their "finest" students were cold-blooded killers.

Columbine High School Principal Frank DeAngelis, who was principal at the time of the shooting, stands at the school's main entrance on April 14, 2004. When Columbine opened its doors that fateful morning, all seemed normal as students went about their daily routines.

Littleton is located in Jefferson County, Colorado. The county is the most populous in the state, with about 525,000 residents. Almost two thousand teenagers from the county attend Columbine High School.[3]

There was nothing unusual about the start of the school day at Columbine on Tuesday morning, April 20, 1999. For some students, the day started very early. Bowling class began at 6:15 A.M. Eric Harris was among the students in the class and arrived at the bowling alley on time. Fellow classmate Jessica Rosecrans did not notice anything unusual about Harris that morning: "He was not acting strange or anything. He was wearing regular clothes. He was wearing flannel."[4]

Student Aaron Hancey normally had choir practice at 7:00 A.M., but like many at Columbine, he was always involved in many activities. Often he had to juggle his schedule. On this morning, he knew he would miss chemistry class because he was in a concert that afternoon. Wanting to get his science work done, he skipped choir and headed for one of the labs. Later, Hancey told a reporter that "it would have been safer if I had been in the choir room."[5]

With graduation just weeks away, most students were focused on finishing up class work and preparing for final exams. By late morning, students could be found just about anywhere on the school grounds. Some wanting quiet went to the school library to study. Others opted to be outside, enjoying the sunny, sixty-degree spring day. It was a nice day to sit under a tree and read a book, eat lunch on the lawn, or head over to the Smoker's Pit for a cigarette break.

At 11:10 A.M., Eric Harris and Dylan Klebold arrived at school in separate cars. Klebold drove his familiar black BMW to the senior parking lot area. Harris pulled his gray Honda Civic into the junior lot, north of where Klebold had parked. They parked their cars so that they flanked the school building. Both Harris and Klebold had missed their earlier classes at Columbine. They had been busy with other things.

In their notebooks, Harris and Klebold had written down detailed descriptions of their plans for April 20, 1999. It was the day they had referred to as "Judgment Day." Their itineraries were very time specific. There was much to do before 11:00 A.M. In Harris's planner, he wrote: "5:00, Get up; 6:00, meet at KS; 7:00, go to Reb's house; 7:15 he leaves to fill propane, I leave to fill gas; 8:30, meet back at his house; 9:00, made d. bag set up car; 9:30, practice gearups; Chill; 10:30, set up four things; 11, go to school; 11:10, set up duffel bags; 11:12, wait near cars, gear up; 11:16, HAHAHA."[6]

For more than a year, Harris and Klebold had been planning to launch a murderous attack on Columbine High School. Hoping to kill as many students as possible, they timed their assault to begin during first period lunch when the cafeteria would be packed with close to five hundred students.

Carrying two huge duffel bags, Harris and Klebold headed for the lunchroom. Inside the bags were two, twenty-pound homemade propane tank bombs. The bombs were timed to explode at 11:17 A.M. As they walked toward the door leading to the cafeteria, Harris saw Brooks Brown, an on-again, off-again friend. Brown had stepped outside to grab

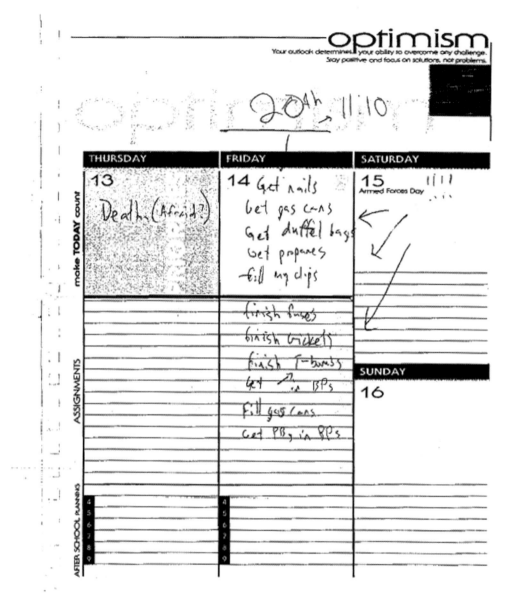

optimism
Your outlook determines your ability to overcome any challenge.
Stay positive and focus on solutions, not problems.

20th, 11:10

THURSDAY	FRIDAY	SATURDAY
13	14 Get nails	15
Death (Afraid?)	Get gas cans	Armed Forces Day
	Get duffel bags	
	Get propanes	
	fill my clips	
	finish fuses	
	finish crickets	
	finish T-bombs	
	get ?? BPs	SUNDAY
	fill gas cans	16
	Get PB, in BPs	

On July 6, 2006, the Jefferson County Sheriff's Office released nearly one thousand pages of documents from the Columbine High School massacre, including essays, schoolwork, and computer files from Eric Harris and Dylan Klebold, the two suicidal killers. No further information has been made available about the contents of the individual documents. In their notebooks, Harris and Klebold wrote detailed descriptions of their plans for April 20, 1999.

a smoke. That cigarette break may have saved his life. As they passed Brown, Harris said, "Brooks, I like you. Get out of here. Go home."[7]

Harris and Klebold then went into the cafeteria. They placed the duffel bags among the countless other backpacks and gym bags lying on the floor around the cafeteria tables and chairs. No one would suspect anything out of the ordinary. Then they went back outside, strapped on their ammunition, put on their black trench coats, and waited for the bombs to detonate.

According to their treacherous plan, they would lie in wait for anyone trying to escape the fiery inferno inside. Armed with shotguns and semiautomatic weapons, Harris and Klebold planned to shoot any survivors fleeing the building.

They waited for a few minutes, but nothing happened. The bombs did not go off. Up in the school library, about four dozen students were using their lunch period to study. In one of the classrooms nearby, Dave Sanders was teaching a class. Farther down the hall, Columbine junior Stephanie Williams was practicing in the choir room. Many students had decided to spend their lunchtime outside and were milling about the grounds.

Suddenly, people in the building became aware of loud popping noises outside. Some thought it was a senior prank. Others thought it was just a video production. Unfortunately, this was no prank or class project. Real bullets were piercing the air. Harris and Klebold had begun their attack, opening fire on their unsuspecting and totally shocked schoolmates.

FATAL FRIENDSHIP

THE NAMES ERIC HARRIS AND DYLAN KLEBOLD will be forever linked. They were best friends. They wanted to be famous. Instead, they achieved infamy. Harris and Klebold will always be remembered for unleashing one of the worst school rampages in American history.

Eric David Harris was born April 9, 1981, in Wichita, Kansas. His father, Wayne, was a decorated officer in the United States Air Force. His mother, Kathy, was a stay-at-home mom, caring for newborn Eric and his three-year-old brother, Kevin.

Because Wayne Harris was in the air force, the family moved often. In 1983, the Harrises moved to Beavercreek, Ohio; in 1989, they moved to Oscoda, Michigan, and in 1992, the family moved to Plattsburgh, New York. Looking back on his childhood, Eric often expressed how difficult it had been for him to start over, trying to fit in and making new friends every time his father was transferred to another base.

Eric Harris (left) and Dylan Klebold are shown in this image made from a video released by the Jefferson County Sheriff's Office as they walk down the hallway of Columbine High School. The video was part of a school project made prior to the shooting.

All the moving around for the Harris family ended in 1993. The government was cutting back on military spending, and slowly bases were being closed across the country. Wayne Harris decided it was time to retire from the air force. The family left New York and moved to Colorado. The Harrises settled down in Littleton.

Wayne Harris got a job training pilots how to fly huge refueling planes. Kathy Harris began working part-time for a catering company. Kevin started his freshman year at Columbine High School. Eric was enrolled at Ken Caryl Middle School. And one of his new classmates was Dylan Klebold.

Born on September 9, 1981, in Denver, Colorado, Dylan Bennett Klebold was the second child of Thomas and Susan. The Klebolds also had another son, Byron, who was three years older than Dylan.

Tom and Susan Klebold were college sweethearts. They had met at Ohio State University. Susan was raised in affluence. Her grandfather, Leo Yassenoff, was a prominent philanthropist and real estate developer. Both of Tom's parents died when he was just a teenager. His older brother raised him.

After college, Tom and Susan Klebold married and moved to the Denver area. Tom got a job as a geophysicist during the boom in the oil business. Susan became a counselor at Arapaho Community College.

As a youngster, Dylan played Little League baseball and joined the Boy Scouts. After second grade, he transferred to Governor's Ranch Elementary School, where he was placed in a program for gifted and talented children. Like Eric Harris, Dylan Klebold spent his middle school years at Ken Caryl. They knew each other and had some of the same friends.

In 1995, Eric Harris and Dylan Klebold enrolled at Columbine High School. It was during their high school years that Harris and Klebold became close friends. Both were interested in video production work and developed strong interests in computers. They worked in the labs, helped to maintain Columbine's computer server, and got involved with the school's Rebel News Network. Klebold had even built his home computer.

Though Harris and Klebold had other friends, they did not fit in with many of their teenage counterparts. However, they had a lot in common. Both were bright and were considered good students. Although Harris was outgoing, Klebold was shy. But they were quite comfortable with each other. They smoked the same cigarettes, were obsessed with the same violent video games, and enjoyed talking endlessly about weapons and explosives.

Harris and Klebold worked at the same place, too, tossing pizzas at Blackjacks. They listened to the same kind of music. One of their favorite bands was Rammstein, a German techno group. Harris was especially intrigued by Nazi culture. Klebold's mother was Jewish, and his classmates said Harris's interest in Nazism made Klebold uncomfortable. However, it did not fracture their friendship.

Harris and Klebold became friends with Chris Morris, a fellow classmate who also worked at Blackjacks. He was rumored to be a member of the "Trench Coat Mafia," a small group of misfits who sometimes wore long black coats. Soon, Harris and Klebold began donning long, black, duster-style trench coats.

Those who knew Harris and Klebold described them as "your average teenagers." What people did not know was that they both had a dark, troubled side. Both harbored a deadly rage that was building daily inside of them.

On January 30, 1998, Harris and Klebold were arrested for breaking into a van and stealing $400 worth of electronic equipment. They were placed in a juvenile diversion program. They were required to pay fines, go to anger management classes, and perform community service. When Harris and Klebold completed the program, all charges against them were dropped, and they were released from the program.

In March 1998, the Jefferson County Sheriff's Office received a complaint about Harris's Internet Web site. The complaint was filed by Judy and Randy Brown, whose son, Brooks, knew Harris and Klebold. The Browns said that Harris was threatening to kill their son. At some point, Harris and Brooks Brown had an argument. Enraged at Brown and all the "uppity" people at school, Harris placed a hate-filled message on his Web site: "I'm coming for EVERYONE soon and I WILL be armed to the . . . teeth and I WILL shoot to kill. . . . I do not care if I live or die in the shoot-out. All I want to do is kill and injure as many of you as I can, especially a few people. Like Brooks Brown."[1]

On his Web site, Harris even included information about various pipe bombs he had made—their size and even their nicknames. Unfortunately, the police department was busy investigating many other crimes, and the sheriff's department never followed up on the Browns' complaint.

In their senior year at Columbine, Harris and Klebold outwardly behaved like regular high school teens. Every day they sat and ate lunch together at the same cafeteria table. They bowled on the same class team. They sat next to each other in their psychology, video production, and creative writing classes. Harris and Klebold also began to make plans for life after high school. Klebold applied to college. Harris filled out an application to enlist in the Marines Corps.

Robyn Anderson, shown here in a video shot by **KUSA-TV** in Denver, Colorado, on April 26, 1999, bought three weapons for Harris and Klebold at a gun show in December 1998.

Harris and Klebold had concealed their plan of assault well. No one knew that they were planning an attack on their high school. Of Harris, friend and fellow student Jennifer LaPlante said, "I think he was the greatest actor I've ever known because he never showed me anything, never deviated from the character I knew—a bright, smiling kid."[2]

Even more disturbing is the fact that the plans had been in the making for a long time. Harris and Klebold had been amassing an arsenal of guns and ammunition for months. In December 1998, Harris, Klebold, and an older friend, Robyn Anderson, went to a gun show. Anderson bought three guns for them—a Hi Point 9-mm carbine rifle and two shotguns. A month later, Harris and Klebold illegally bought a TEC-DC9 semiautomatic pistol from Mark Manes, an acquaintance from Blackjacks.

On weekends, the boys spent hours in Harris's garage making pipe bombs and Molotov cocktails. Klebold even carved his nickname "voDKa" on some of the pipe bombs. At some point, they constructed two large propane-tank bombs that could kill hundreds of people.

As Graduation Day approached, Harris and Klebold went about their normal routines. On March 4, they had their class picture taken. On the evening of April 9, Klebold and Anderson met Harris at the local bowling alley to celebrate his eighteenth birthday.

Klebold had been accepted at the University of Arizona. A week before the shooting, Klebold and his father toured the university's Tucson campus. Tom Klebold even put down a deposit on a dorm room for his son.

While Klebold was in Tucson, Harris was getting bad news from the Marine Corps. They had rejected Harris's application because he was on an antidepressant medication. He would have to be off the drug for six months before he could reapply.

Saturday evening, April 17, was senior prom night. Klebold went with his friend Robyn Anderson. Harris did not have a date, but showed up at the after-prom party at Columbine's gymnasium. On Monday, April 19, Harris and Klebold went to school but left before their last class of the day. That night, Harris picked up one hundred rounds of ammunition that Manes had purchased for him.

Mark Manes (left), with his parents, Diann and Mike Manes, appears at the Jefferson County Courthouse on August 18, 1999, after pleading guilty to weapons charges. Manes illegally sold a semiautomatic pistol to Eric Harris and Dylan Klebold before the shooting at Columbine High School.

At 11:10 A.M. on Tuesday morning, April 20, Harris and Klebold maneuvered their cars into the student parking lot. In a few minutes, the school cafeteria would be packed with hundreds of students. For Harris and Klebold, what they had identified as "Judgment Day" in their journals and videotapes was about to begin.

CHAPTER THREE

RAMPAGE IN THE HIGH SCHOOL

WHILE HARRIS AND KLEBOLD were arriving at the school's parking lots, students were going from one class to another or were heading to the school cafeteria for lunch. Rachel Scott and Richard Castaldo decided to eat outside. They were sitting together on the grass on the upper level near the west entrance. A few minutes later, students Daniel Rohrbough, Sean Graves, and Lance Kirklin were coming outside through the lower-level door of the cafeteria. They were on their way over to the Smoker's Pit at Clement Park. Mark Taylor and Michael Johnson were sitting in a group of five students on the grass, just west of the lower-level stairs, near the entrance to the cafeteria.

At 11:19 A.M., someone heard Harris or Klebold shout, "Go! Go!"[1] Both then pulled out guns from underneath their trench coats and opened fire. They were also toting duffel bags stuffed with homemade pipe bombs.

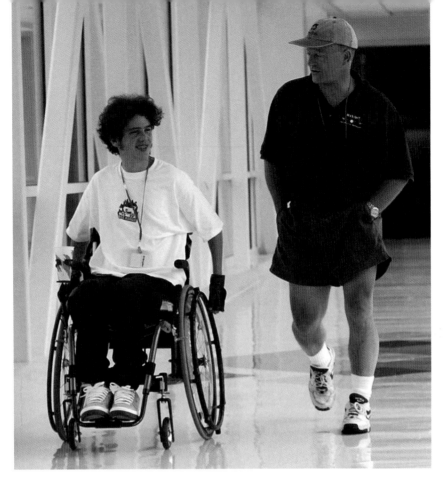

Richard Castaldo and his father, Rick, are shown in this photo taken August 4, 1999. Castaldo, one of the first students assaulted at Columbine High School, was severely injured by eight gunshot wounds. He survived the attack, but was paralyzed from the chest down.

Harris and Klebold fired their first shots where Scott and Castaldo were sitting. Scott was killed. Castaldo sustained severe injuries from eight bullet wounds. Harris next fired at Rohrbough, Graves, and Kirklin as they emerged from the cafeteria. All three were wounded. Graves, who was shot in the back, dragged himself back through the cafeteria door.

The five students sitting on the grass on the west side of the stairs were sprayed with bullets. Two were wounded. Johnson was bleeding badly from being shot in the leg. He managed to reach an athletic storage shed and take cover with other students. Taylor was too badly wounded to move.

Klebold went down the ramp to the cafeteria. When he reached Rohrbough, he shot him again, killing him. Then, Klebold stood over Kirklin and shot him in the face. Stepping over Graves in the doorway, Klebold briefly went into the cafeteria.

A few moments later, Klebold rejoined Harris outside on the upper level. Student Anne Marie Hochhalter, who was running toward the cafeteria, was shot several times and fell to the ground. Witnesses told police they heard one of the killers say, "This is what we always wanted to do. This is awesome."[2] Students also reported seeing Harris and Klebold lighting and tossing pipe bombs and Molotov cocktails on the roof, toward the parking lots, and onto the grassy areas of the school.

At 11:24 A.M., teacher Dave Sanders ran into the cafeteria to warn students of the grave danger. He yelled for everybody to get down and take cover. Steve Cohen and his sister, Diana, were in the cafeteria when Sanders ran in. Steve Cohen said later: "The first thing that came to my mind was the school shootings in Kentucky and Mississippi, so I thought, 'Oh, my God, we have to get out of here!' We all ran up the main stairwell, and Diana fell and got kind of trampled. It was chaos. Hundreds of people. I looked behind me, and she was gone. I was just standing there looking around for Diana. And my friend was yelling at me, 'You've got to go! You've got to go!'"[3]

Students ran in every direction—toward the building exits, to nearby classrooms, into offices, closets, bathrooms—anywhere to escape or hide. Nineteen-year-old Adam Foss and some of his schoolmates barricaded themselves in the choir room office: "We closed the door, and me and two buddies put the desk in front of it. We were, like, 'They can shoot all they want, but they are not coming in.'"[4]

Local police received a 911 call at 11:23 A.M. Neil Gardner, Jefferson County sheriff's deputy and school resource officer, was eating lunch near the Smoker's Pit. He also received a call on the school's radio. One of the custodians was alerting him to serious trouble at the south side of the high school.

When Gardner got there, he saw Harris firing his rifle into the glass doors of the upper entrance. Inside, teacher Patti Nielson and student Brian Anderson were heading toward the doors. Metal fragments and shards of glass hit them when the doors shattered from the impact. Though wounded, Nielson and Anderson managed to retreat to the library. Nielson implored the students already in the room to get down and seek cover under the library tables. Nielson herself hid under the front counter and called 911 at 11:25 A.M. The commotion was so loud that the dispatchers could hear the gunfire and explosions through the telephone receiver.

Outside, Gardner and Harris exchanged gunfire before Harris and Klebold disappeared inside the school. Gardner radioed for assistance.

Inside the building, Harris and Klebold tossed lit pipe bombs in the corridors and continued to fire their weapons at fleeing students. Bullets ricocheted off lockers, and smoke from the pipe bombs filled the air.

While Harris and Klebold were firing their guns down the main hallway, teacher Dave Sanders was still helping students escape. As he turned the corner from the stairwell into the hallway outside the library, he was hit by a shotgun blast. He fell immediately to the floor. Colleague Richard Long helped Sanders into Science Room 3.

In another lab room across the hall, student Aaron Hancey was trying to

Dave Sanders, the only teacher murdered during the rampage at Columbine, was gunned down as he tried to help students escape.

hide from the attack. He had been working on his science project when he suddenly heard gunfire. Looking out one of the lab windows, he saw students running from the building. He was terrified by the shotgun blasts. "I could feel it through the walls. With each one, I could feel the walls move," he said.[5] When science teacher Kent Friesen ran in and asked if anyone knew first aid, Hancey said yes. They then sprinted across the hallway to Science Room 3, where about thirty students had taken refuge. Sanders was lying on the floor bleeding heavily.

In this photo made from security camera footage, Eric Harris (left) and Dylan Klebold are seen carrying their weapons in the cafeteria during the shooting rampage.

Hancey and student Kevin Starkey began administering first aid to Sanders. They were trying to stop the bleeding. Students talked to Sanders. They found his wallet and took out pictures of his wife and daughters and showed them to him. They tried to keep him alert. One student placed a sign in the lab room window, "I'm Bleeding to Death," so police would know where to send emergency help.

While SWAT (Special Weapons and Tactics) teams, police, and rescue personnel converged outside the school, Harris and Klebold continued their rampage inside. They entered the library. Nielson, another teacher, and fifty-six students had taken refuge there. Most students had already listened to Nielson and were hiding underneath the tables. It was 11:29 A.M., only twelve minutes after the shooting began.

Witnesses said that Harris or Klebold yelled "Get up! Everyone with a white cap or a baseball cap, stand up." Others thought they heard "All jocks stand up. We'll get the guys in the white hats." No one in the library moved. At that point, one of the gunmen said, "Fine, I'll start shooting."[6] Students heard Harris pump a round into his shotgun. He then fired several rounds down the length of the front counter. The hail of bullets injured Evan Todd, who had been crouched behind a copying machine.

Klebold and Harris walked toward the library windows. Kyle Velasquez was the only person in the library who had not tried to hide. He was sitting at a computer table. Klebold shot him as he walked by, killing him.

Harris and Klebold put down their backpacks and turned to look out the library windows. Harris fired shots from the window at fleeing students and police officers below. Klebold took off his trench coat and briefly joined Harris.

Nielson dropped the phone on which she had dialed 911 and sought better cover under a desk. For the next seven and a half minutes, dispatchers heard the carnage as it unfolded—how the gunmen taunted and executed students trapped in the library—with no rhyme or reason.

Those hiding under a cluster of tables closest to the windows were the gunmen's next targets. Klebold turned and shot at table 15, under which were Daniel Steepleton, Makai Hall, and Patrick Ireland. All three were wounded. Harris wandered over to a computer table where Steven Curnow and Kacey Reugsegger were huddled together. Harris fired beneath the table killing Curnow and wounding Reugsegger. Moving to where two girls were hiding under table 19, Harris slapped the tabletop twice, said "Peek-a-boo,"and then fired under the table.[7] Cassie Bernall was mortally wounded. The recoil from the gun hit Harris in the face, breaking his nose.

Bree Pasquale, who was sitting in the open on the floor near the windows, noticed blood running from Harris's nose after he shot Bernall. She thought Harris seemed dazed as he walked over to her and asked her if she wanted to die. Harris undoubtedly would have shot Pasquale, but Klebold interrupted him. Klebold was standing over table 16, where Matthew Kechter and Isaiah Shoels had taken cover. Shoels, who was African American, became the target of Klebold's racial slurs.

Joining Klebold, Harris was heard laughing, saying "Everyone's gonna die. We're gonna blow up the school anyway."[8] He then fired his shotgun under the table, killing Shoels. Klebold, who was standing on the other side of the table, fired, killing Kechter.

Harris paused to light an explosive and rolled it toward the wounded Steepleton, Hall, and Ireland. Hall grabbed the explosive and threw it to the corner of the library. Though it exploded, no one was injured.

For the next few minutes, Harris and Klebold seemed to wander aimlessly through the library. Harris went toward several rows of bookcases. Klebold walked toward the library entrance. Harris jumped up on some bookshelves and shook them, then disappeared between them. Klebold aimed his shotgun at a display cabinet. In a heavy barrage of gunfire the cabinet was destroyed. Then the killing resumed.

Emergency personnel assist student Patrick Ireland as he attempts to escape through a library window during the shooting rampage. Klebold and Harris moved from table to table in the library, killing and wounding many students.

The gunmen's next victims were close by, hiding under a group of tables near the library entrance.

Klebold shot at table 1 just behind the display cabinet, injuring Mark Kintgen. Turning left, Klebold fired again, hitting Valeen Schnurr and Lisa Kreutz under table 2. Shooting as fast as the gun would fire, Klebold killed Lauren Townsend.

Harris returned and taunted a few students behind table 2 before heading to the next table. There, he shot Nicole Nowlen and John Tomlin. Wounded, Tomlin tried to come out from under the table. Klebold shot him again, killing him.

Harris turned back toward table 2, where three students had already been shot. He fired again, killing Kelly Fleming. Townsend and Kreutz were hit again. Another student crouched with the group, Jeanna Park, was injured.

Harris and Klebold paused in their killing spree to reload their weapons at a table in the center of the library. Harris noticed a student under a nearby table. Told to identify himself, John Savage, an acquaintance of Klebold, asked him what they were doing. Klebold answered, "Oh, just killing people."[9] He then told Savage to get out of the library.

In the remaining few minutes of terror, Harris and Klebold shot four more students. Harris killed Daniel Mauser. Both gunmen then fired under the last table they would attack, injuring Jennifer Doyle and Austin Eubanks. The gunfire killed Corey DePooter, the last student Harris and Klebold shot. Incredibly, it was only 11:35 A.M.—just sixteen minutes after their shooting spree had begun.

Harris and Klebold left the library and wandered the halls of the school. They lit more pipe bombs and tossed them randomly. Surviving students in the library fled through an emergency exit door. Evan Todd, though wounded himself, carried Mark Kintgen outside to the athletic equipment shed. There he administered first aid to Kintgen and to Michael Johnson, who had been wounded earlier.

A surveillance camera videotape captured Harris and Klebold returning to the cafeteria at 11:44 A.M. Disappointed that the propane bombs had not detonated, Harris fired his weapon at one of them.

A mother embraces her daughter after they are reunited following the shooting at Columbine High School. The rampage ended at 12:08 P.M. when Harris and Klebold took their own lives.

Klebold lobbed a pipe bomb over to the tank, but it still did not ignite. They lit several other bombs, and a small fire finally erupted.

It is not clear what Harris and Klebold did over the next few minutes, though they were seen again on the cafeteria videotape at 11:57 A.M. The propane tanks sat idle, and the sprinkler system had extinguished the fire. The gunmen returned to the library, where they exchanged gunfire with law enforcement officers and paramedics outside. This exchange occurred between 12:02 P.M. and 12:05 P.M., while paramedics were attempting to reach wounded students. At 12:08 P.M., Harris and Klebold turned their weapons on themselves, committing suicide. It would be hours before police and rescue teams would know for certain that the violent rampage had ended.

WAR ZONE

WHEN THE SHOOTING FINALLY ENDED, fifteen people, including the two gunmen, were dead. Another twenty-three suffered various injuries. Some of the wounded were in grave condition when they arrived at hospitals around the Littleton area. Although many of the injuries were serious, all of the wounded survived.

Despite the chaos around them, rescue personnel were able to reach most of the injured students. Some were treated on the spot. The more seriously wounded, like Richard Castaldo, Lance Kirklin, and Sean Graves, were evacuated to area hospitals. Anxious parents, brothers, sisters, and schoolmates assembled at Leawood Elementary School. There they waited for word on the condition of students and faculty injured or missing.

By the time police teams entered the school, the murderous assault was over. Police did not know then that the gunmen were dead. Because they were unaware that the immediate danger had passed, precious time

Fran Allison, right, comforts her daughter Brooke, left, after the shooting at Columbine High School. Students, faculty, and their families assembled in nearby Leawood Elementary School to await word on the condition of wounded or missing victims.

was spent on devising a tactical plan. No one outside the building knew how many gunmen there were or exactly where they were. Information was literally jamming emergency phone lines. Teachers and students flooded 911 with calls. Some reported that Harris and Klebold were in the library. Others told dispatchers that the gunmen were in the cafeteria. The fire alarms wailed through the halls. It was impossible to follow the sounds of gunfire.

Proceeding carefully, SWAT teams entered the school through entrances farthest away from where most of the attack seemed to be centered. No one was actually prepared for what they saw as they moved through the hallways and stairwells. The building was filled with smoke. Water from the emergency sprinkler system dampened the walls and floors. Ceiling tiles were loose. Rounds of live ammunition and spent bullet casings littered the floor. Nails and glass from exploded bombs were embedded in the walls. Extinguished pipe bombs lay on top of burned carpeting.

Slowly, SWAT teams searched each hallway, closet, bathroom, and crawl space, looking for signs of the killers and other dangers. Sergeant Allen Simmons led the first SWAT team inside. "Every time we came around a corner," Simmons later recalled, "we didn't know what was waiting for us."[1]

Once an area was safely secured, students found hiding were evacuated. It took the SWAT teams more than two hours to reach teacher Dave Sanders. Another two hours passed before a paramedic reached Science Room 3. Despite the valiant efforts of students and teachers to keep Sanders alive, he died before professional medical help arrived. He was the last fatality.

Ironically, the last area that the police reached was the library. It was 3:22 P.M. Officers observed more "gunshot holes in the windows, bomb fragments and shrapnel on the floor . . . and a pipe bomb embedded in the wall just outside the library."[2]

Anyone still in the library able to leave under his or her own power was escorted out of

Members of a SWAT team march to Columbine High School as they prepare to do a final search. It took police and rescue personnel hours to search the school and evacuate all the students and faculty.

the building. Officials combed the library, searching for signs of life. One student, Patrick Ireland, had not waited for help. Ireland was suffering from two shotgun wounds to the head. Somehow he made his way to the shattered library windows and began lowering himself out. Rescue teams spotted him in time to move a vehicle near the window and catch him as he fell.

Paramedics evacuated Lisa Kreutz from the library, while officers assisted Patti Nielson and three other women to safety. Police discovered the bodies of Harris and Klebold. Both appeared to have died from self-inflicted gunshot wounds to the head.

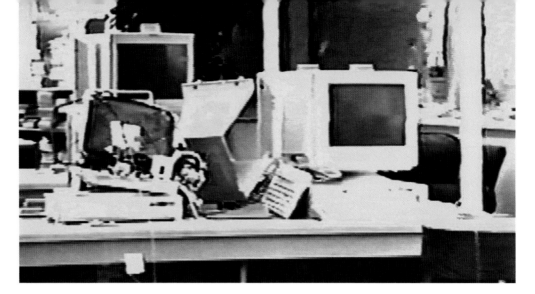

The library, the final area reached by law enforcement, looked like a war zone. This photo taken from a video shows computers destroyed and shattered windows. Ten of the twelve students killed during the shooting were murdered in the library.

Next came the grim task of identifying the dead. Because there were so many bombs, weapons, and so much ammunition scattered throughout the library and the rest of the school, law enforcement officials declared the building unsafe. Until bomb squads could go through the backpacks, hallways, and classrooms to disarm or detonate the bombs, no one was allowed to enter the building.

It was not until the next day that the bodies of the thirteen victims and the two gunmen were removed from the school. Students Rachel Scott and Daniel Rohrbough had been killed outside. The students who died in the library massacre were Cassie Bernall, Steven Curnow, Corey DePooter, Kelly Fleming, Matthew Kechter, Daniel Mauser, Isaiah Shoels, John Tomlin, Lauren Townsend, and Kyle Velasquez. Dave Sanders was the only teacher killed.

HORROR, TEARS, AND HEALING

IN THE DAYS FOLLOWING THE MASSACRE, people were in shock. Tears flowed endlessly. Intense sadness hung over the whole community. Many people were outraged and angry that something like this could happen.

Impromptu memorials to the slain victims appeared almost overnight. Lauren Townsend's car remained where she parked it on the morning of April 20. The next day, flowers, notes, and prayers covered it. Crosses for the victims were erected on a hill on the Columbine grounds.

Five days after the shooting, more than seventy thousand mourners gathered to honor and remember the thirteen victims. Vice President Al Gore was among those who came to express his sorrow and comfort the grieving. He said, "To all the families of those who died here, I say

Two unidentified mourners stop to view the display of flowers, cards, and balloons left at a makeshift memorial in Clement Park near Columbine High School. Five days after the shooting, more than seventy thousand people gathered to honor and remember the victims.

you are not alone. The heart of America aches with yours. We hold your agony in the center of our prayers. The entire nation is a community of shock, of love, of grief."[1]

The Littleton community said its good-byes and buried its dead. Most Columbine students wanted their lives to get back to as close to normal as possible. Eventually, all of the seriously wounded students were able to leave the hospital.

May 22, 1999, was Graduation Day at Columbine High School. Four hundred and forty students entered Fiddler's Green Amphitheater wearing the blue and gold colors of their school. Wounded students Lisa Kreutz and Jeanna Park proudly wore their National Honor Society gold collars. Kreutz rolled up in her wheelchair to accept her diploma. Park had been shot in the right knee, left foot, and right shoulder. She had this to say about attending the ceremony: "I was just glad to be at graduation. At first the doctors weren't even sure I could walk. It was exciting enough to just be able to walk up and get my diploma."[2]

There was a moment of silence for two seniors who would not graduate with the rest—Lauren Townsend and Isaiah Shoels. Those in attendance also paused to remember slain teacher Dave Sanders. Later in the ceremony, Townsend's parents received a moving ovation from the audience as they accepted their daughter's valedictorian honors and diploma. Graduation Day for the class of 1999 should have been joyous. Instead, it was bittersweet.

As the Columbine community tried to get past the tragedy, investigators began to piece together what happened. Over the next eight months, a task force of more than eighty detectives worked on the case. They conducted interviews with 4,500 witnesses and gathered 10,000 pieces of evidence collected at the school and from the homes of Harris and Klebold.[3] The official Jefferson County Sheriff's Department report was released to the public in May 2000.

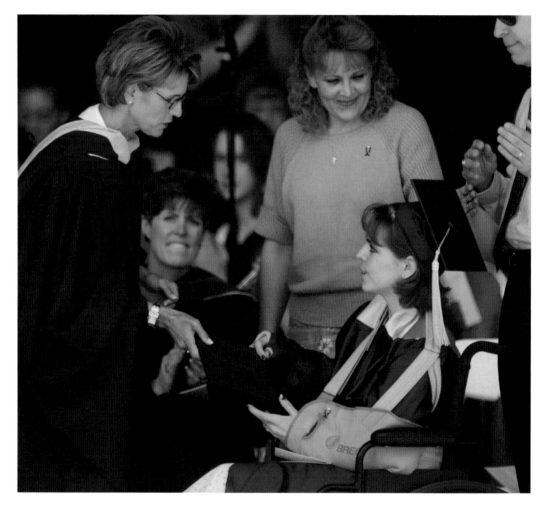

Columbine High School senior Lisa Kreutz (in wheelchair), who had been wounded during the shooting, is presented her diploma by school administrator Barb Monseu at graduation ceremonies on May 22, 1999.

Among the evidence found at the killers' homes were the boys' journals and five videotapes they recorded before the massacre. On the tapes, Harris and Klebold revealed their deep-seated hatred of life and their goal to kill as many people as possible.

To prepare for "Judgment Day," Harris and Klebold acquired enough guns and ammunition to kill many more people than they did on April 20, 1999. They constructed a total of ninety-five bombs of various types and sizes. Harris and Klebold heaved six of them in the cafeteria and six in classrooms and the hallways. Five of the devices were detonated in the library, and thirteen were tossed about outside. Had the two propane-tank bombs exploded, the consequences would have been catastrophic.

The gunmen placed bombs in their own cars and left a diversionary bomb off campus. This bomb was intended to draw police to an area away from the school. This was to keep police occupied while Harris and Klebold played out their murderous attack. What investigators discovered was that the killers' plan went amiss because the propane bombs did not detonate. Instead, they improvised by unleashing a random shooting assault.

Many believed that Harris was the leader and Klebold the follower. Student after student interviewed said that Klebold could not have been a party to such madness. News reporters on the scene asked who the shooters might be. Someone mentioned Klebold's name. A reporter scribbled it down on his pad. Senior Chris Hooker told him, "You'd better cross Dylan's name off. He's not that kind of person. He would never do this."[4] Sixteen-year-old Jacob Cary agreed: "No way he'd do that on his own. He's not a leader in any way. He was just a nice guy, if you got to know him."[5]

Even before the official report was released, families of the slain and wounded began leveling harsh criticism at the way Sheriff John Stone's department handled the crisis. Evan Todd's father felt the police waited too long. "When 500 officers go to a battle zone, and not one comes away with a scratch, then something's wrong. I expected dead officers, crippled officers, disfigured officers—not just children and teachers."[6] Dave Sanders's daughter, Angela, raised similar doubts. It had taken SWAT teams almost three hours to reach her dying father. She asked, "How many of those kids could have lived if they had moved more quickly? This is what I do every day. I sit and ponder, 'What if.'"[7]

On January 28, 2000, Colorado governor Bill Owens appointed his own commission to look into the Columbine tragedy. The ultimate purpose of the commission was to make recommendations on how to prevent such an attack from happening again. The commission was also charged with providing better ways to handle similar situations in the future.

The final report was released on May 17, 2001. Aside from the expected recommendations, the commission was also very critical of the Jefferson County officials "who failed to look seriously at a 'massive' number of clues to the intentions of Eric Harris and Dylan Klebold."[8] Commission chairman William Erickson said, "We had all this information, and nobody acted upon it."[9] Undoubtedly, Erickson was referring

As the families of the slain and the wounded began to heal, the Columbine community came together to rebuild the school. The new HOPE Columbine Memorial Library is shown in this photo on April 15, 2004.

not only to the complaint filed by the Browns about Harris's threats, but also the boys' juvenile records, and their violent school essays and video productions.

Since the Columbine tragedy, dozens of lawsuits have been filed against the county and the parents of Eric Harris and Dylan Klebold. Mark Manes was sentenced to six years in prison for illegally selling the TEC-DC9 semiautomatic handgun Klebold used in the killing spree.

The wounded continue to heal. They have moved on with their lives. Some went on to college and now have successful careers. Patrick Ireland, a field director for Northwestern Mutual Financial Network in Denver, gives speeches about his experiences during the shooting. Sean Graves is a spokesman for the Christopher and Dana Reeve

Family and friends gather at a candlelight vigil at the Columbine High School Memorial in Clement Park on April 19, 2009, the day before the tenth anniversary of the shooting. The memorial honors the victims of the tragedy, but also serves as a grim reminder of the consequences of student violence.

Foundation, which advocates for research and improving the quality of life for those with spinal cord injuries.[10]

Memorial funds have been established in the memories of the victims. In June 2001, the public got its first glimpse of the new HOPE Columbine Memorial Library. The $3.1 million needed to build the new library and atrium was raised by HOPE (Healing of People Everywhere). Fund-raisers included parents of some of the Columbine victims. There is also the 1.4-acre Columbine Memorial in Clement Park located next to the school. It was unveiled on September 21, 2007.

Despite the horrific events at Columbine High School on April 20, 1999, deaths resulting from school violence are rare. However, gun violence, especially with young people and in schools, is a serious issue.

On April 16, 2007, another tragedy brought this issue back into focus for all Americans. At Virginia Tech, a college in Blacksburg, Virginia, senior student, Seung Hui-Cho, went on a rampage killing thirty-two students and professors before taking his own life.

Incidents such as these prompt educators, law enforcement, and parents to address the problem of student violence more thoroughly. New methods have been developed to train law enforcement officials to better execute response and rescue efforts. Programs have been introduced in schools to educate students about peer violence, to develop better tolerance for others, and to incorporate safe communication to alert adults to potential problems before they happen. Parents have been encouraged to be more involved with their children on a day-to-day basis, including knowing who their children's friends are, how they are doing in school, and how they spend their free time. By involving everyone in the process, educators, parents, and students hope to make our schools safer and happier places.

CHAPTER NOTES

CHAPTER 1. "JUDGMENT DAY"

1. Nancy Gibbs, "In Sorrow and Disbelief," *Time*, May 3, 1999, p. 2.

2. Ibid.

3. "Jefferson County, Colorado, State & County QuickFacts," U.S. Census Bureau, October 13, 2011, <http://quickfacts.census.gov/qfd/states/08/08059.html> (October 25, 2011).

4. Lisa Ryckman and Mike Anton, "Mundane Gave Way to Madness," *RockyMountainNews.com*, April 25, 1999, <http://denver.rockymountainnews.com/shooting/0425xsho1.shtml> (April 20, 2001).

5. Ibid.

6. "Jefferson County Sheriff's Office report, Columbine High School Shootings," *Jefferson County Public Library*, April 20, 1999, <http://info.jefferson.lib.co.us/columbine-cd.htm> (May 16, 2000).

7. Ibid.

CHAPTER 2. FATAL FRIENDSHIP

1. Nancy Gibbs and Timothy Roche, "The Columbine Tapes," *Time*, December 20, 1999, pp. 40–51.

2. Bill Briggs and Jason Blevins, "A Boy With Many Sides," *Denver Post.com*, May 2, 1999, <http://www.denverpost.com/news/shot0502b.htm> (May 23, 2000).

CHAPTER 3. RAMPAGE IN THE HIGH SCHOOL

1. "Jefferson County Sheriff's Office report, Columbine High School Shootings," *Jefferson County Public Library*, April 20, 1999, <http://info.jefferson.lib.co.us/columbine-cd.htm> (May 16, 2000).

2. Ibid.

3. Tod Olson and John DiConsiglio, "A School Under Siege," *Teen People*, August 1999, pp. 118–122.

4. Ibid.

5. Lisa Ryckman and Mike Anton, "Mundane Gave Way to Madness," *RockyMountainNews.com,* April 25, 1999, <http://denver.rockymountainnews.com/shooting/0425xsho1.shtml> (April 20, 2001).

6. "Jefferson County Sheriff's Office report, Columbine High School Shootings."

7. "The Report of Governor Bill Owens' Columbine Review Commission," *State of Colorado Homepage*, May 2001, <http://www.state.co.us/columbine/> (May 17, 2001).

8. "Jefferson County Sheriff's Office report, Columbine High School Shootings."

9. "The Report of Governor Bill Owens' Columbine Review Commission."

CHAPTER 4. WAR ZONE

1. Nancy Gibbs and Timothy Roche, "The Columbine Tapes," *Time*, December 20, 1999, pp. 40–51.

2. "The Report of Governor Bill Owens' Columbine Review Commission," *State of Colorado Homepage*, May 2001, <http://www.state.co.us/columbine/> (May 17, 2001).

CHAPTER 5. HORROR, TEARS, AND HEALING

1. Kristin Dizon and Jason Hickman, "Columbine Victims Remembered," *TheDailyCamera.com*, April 26, 1999, <http://www.thedailycamera.com/shooting/26amem.html> (June 12, 2001).

2. Mike Soraghan, Susan Greene, Beth DeFalco, Mike McPhee, and Andrew Guy, "Columbine Graduation Day," *DistributionConcepts.com*, May 23, 1999, <http://www.distributionconcepts.com/grad.htm> (June 12, 2001).

3. Charley Able and Peggy Lowe, "Report: 6 Shot in First Minutes," *RockyMountainNews.com*, May 10, 2000, <http://denver.rockymountainnews.com/shooting/0510repr1.shtml> (June 12, 2001)

4. Kevin Simpson, Patricia Callahan, and Peggy Lowe, "Life and Death of a Follower," *DenverPost.com*, May 2, 1999, <http://www.denverpost.com/news/shot0502c.htm> (May 23, 2000).

5. Ibid.

6. Nancy Gibbs and Timothy Roche, "The Columbine Tapes," *Time*, December 20, 1999, pp. 40–51.

7. Ibid.

8. "A Preventable Tragedy," *TheDailyCamera.com*, May 2, 2001, <http://www.bouldernews.com/opinion/editrials/02eedit.html> (June 12, 2001).

9. Ibid.

10. "Columbine: Where are they now," *The Denver Post*, April 19, 2009, <http://www.denverpost.com/ci_12174129> (October 25, 2011).

GLOSSARY

affluence—A condition of having much wealth or property.

antidepressant—Medication used to relieve mental depression.

arsenal—A collection of weapons.

barricade—To prevent access by placing an obstacle or barrier in the way.

carnage—A massacre, or mass killing, of living things.

corridor—A passageway or hallway that leads to rooms, like classrooms in a school.

cul-de-sac—A street closed at one end.

detonate—To set off an explosion, like a bomb.

dispatcher—A communications operator for police, firefighters, or taxicabs.

extinguish—To put out something burning, like a fire.

flank—A position at the side of something.

geophysicist—One who studies the processes and occurrences of Earth.

impromptu—Spontaneous; not prepared ahead of time.

infamy—Achieving an evil reputation.

Molotov cocktail—A crude bomb made by using a bottle filled with gasoline and a wick.

ovation—An expression of approval; enthusiastic applause.

philanthropist—One who performs a charitable act.

rampage—A course of violent or reckless action or behavior.

ricochet—To bounce off at an angle.

surveillance—Keeping a close watch on someone or something.

SWAT—Special Weapons and Tactics.

tactic—A planned action for a particular purpose.

valedictorian—The student with the highest academic rank in a graduating class. Usually, the valedictorian gives the commencement address at graduation.

FURTHER READING

BOOKS

Brezina, Corona. *Deadly School and Campus Violence.* New York: Rosen Publishing Group, 2009.

Cullen, Dave. *Columbine.* New York: Twelve, 2009.

MacKay, Jenny. *The Columbine School Shooting.* Detroit: Lucent Books, 2010.

Marsico, Katie. *The Columbine High School Massacre: Murder in the Classroom.* Tarrytown, N.Y.: Marshall Cavendish Benchmark, 2011.

Simons, Rae. *Students in Danger: Survivors of School Violence.* Broomall, Pa.: Mason Crest Publishers, 2009.

INTERNET ADDRESSES

Centers for Disease Control and Prevention (CDC): School Violence
<http://www.cdc.gov/violenceprevention/youthviolence/schoolviolence/>

Columbine Memorial
<http://www.columbinememorial.org/default.asp>

National Center for Children Exposed to Violence: School Violence
<http://www.nccev.org/violence/school.html#websites>

INDEX